Insights on Prayer

Lisa Marshall

DEDICATION

This book is dedicated to my mentor Thetus Tenney.
Thank you for teaching me so much about prayer and
prayer ministry. Your investment in my life and ministry
has had a profound impact. I love and appreciate you.

CONTENTS

1 I NEED YOU, YOU NEED ME

Are you familiar with the Hezekiah Walker song, "I Need You to Survive"? It is the modern day version of "You're My Brother, You're My Sister." The message is the same—we need each other. We are the body of Christ. While we all have different parts to play in the body, all parts are needed to make the body whole and complete. So in a sense, what happens to you happens to me. If you have a problem, I indirectly have one too.

A line in the song says *"I'll pray for you, you pray for me. I love you, I need you to survive."*

I wonder how different things would be if we prayed for one another on a daily basis? You see, no matter how talented and dedicated, no one person has every gift needed. It takes us all working together. If we truly love our neighbor as ourselves, then shouldn't as much of our time spent in prayer be praying for the success and blessings of others as for ourselves?

So if we are the body, it would stand to reason that if you have a problem, I have one too—and if you succeed, so do I.

Find someone to partner with in prayer. Pray for his or her success and pray blessings into the person's life. By doing this you may very well pray success and blessings into your own life as well.

2 KINGDOM PRAYING

Have you ever analyzed your prayers? Are they more selfish than selfless? The truth is, for the typical believer the majority of time in prayer is spent focused on self. "God bless me, my family, my health, my bank account, my happiness, and my pleasure." We are like one young lady who prayed, "Lord, I ask nothing for myself, but please send my mother a fine, handsome son-in-law."

Certainly God can and does bless us in all these areas and more, but when this is the exclusive focus of our prayers, it reflects that we have lost sight of some very valuable principals of prayer.

"God, what can I do for You?" Too often we have a shopping list mentality, coming to God to get things rather than coming to get God Himself and seek His will. How many times do we come to God and simply ask, "God, what can I do for You today, or what would You have me pray for?"

In the Sermon on the Mount, Christ taught His disciples to pray *"Your kingdom come,"* and to *"seek first His kingdom and His righteousness, and all these things will be given to you as well" (Matthew 6:10, 33).* Kingdom-focused prayers end not in my success and happiness, but in the building of God's kingdom and the power of His righteousness in the lives of His children. Jesus said this type of praying would result in God adding to us all these things.

3 DO YOU WORRY ON YOUR KNEES?

While driving one night, I noticed the sign in front of a church near my house. It said, "Do you pray or just worry on your knees?" I jotted it down, thinking it would be a great quote to use at some point in the future. However, the more I got to thinking about it, the more it spoke to me.

If we are really honest, how often are we guilty of getting down to pray and telling God how bad things are, or how we don't know how in the world this can ever *"work together for good"*? Now, I am not making light of or downplaying serious problems and situations that are in dire need of divine intervention. However, I think we sometimes forget how powerful God is.

Do your prayers sound like audible worrying or like a resounding declaration of the power and confidence in the God you serve?

Something to think about.

DO YOU PRAY OR JUST
WORRY ON YOUR KNEES?

4 PRAYING THE WORD

Prayer is not for the purpose of getting everything we want from God. Prayer is the way God gets His will done on this earth.

To a large extent, our all-powerful God has chosen to limit His power to the prayers of His people.

"And we can be confident that He will listen to us whenever we ask Him for anything in line with His will. And if we know He is listening when we make our requests, we can be sure He will give us what we ask for" (*1 John 5:14, 15* NLT).

How do we know what God's will is? We can be confident that God's will is contained in the pages of His Word. Praying the Word is praying powerfully and totally in the will of God. It is almost as though we can step into God's mind, or His thoughts, and pray according to His will, knowing He will hear us.

The most powerful thing a Christian can do is pray the Word of God.

"In the beginning was the Word and the Word was with God and the Word was God" (John 1:1).

When we pray the Word, we are praying God Himself right into the middle of the situation.

Suddenly, our prayers go from pitiful, desperate cries to powerful prayers of authority!

Practice praying the Word. The Word is forever settled and cannot fail.

5 GOD'S TIMING

I remember it well. I had just spent what seemed like hours praying. It was probably more like five minutes, but for a kid my age, that was a long time. As I got up, weary from my time of intercession, my granny looked at me and asked in a way that only Gran could, "Do you think your prayers made it to the ceiling?"

I cannot begin to tell you how many times since that day I have wondered the same thing. Has anyone besides me ever felt like your prayers weren't going anywhere? You pray and nothing happens. You remind God that you belong to Him and the Bible says to *"Ask and ye shall receive"*—as if He didn't already know—still, nothing. What do you do?

Consider when your car doesn't start. You turn the key and nothing happens. Do you keep doing this for days, or do you try to find the problem? You can turn the key all day every day, but if there is a mechanical problem, you will be sitting in the same place a year later getting the same result. Would it not make sense to have a mechanic find what is wrong?

Keep in mind that God's timing isn't always our timing. Actually, I have found God's time is very seldom my timing, but He's God and He's good at it, so I will trust Him.

There are times it isn't time and there are times it isn't working. If it isn't time, ask God to help you while you wait. If it isn't working, perhaps it is time to change your approach.

6 WE CAN ALL PRAY

Only once in Scripture does Jesus give a prayer request. Only once do we find that He asked His believers to pray specifically for something. Nowhere did He ask us to pray for the harvest to bring forth much fruit. Rather He said, "*The harvest is truly plenteous, but the labourers are few; pray ye therefore the Lord of the harvest, that He will send forth labourers into His harvest.*"

The church has been commissioned to go and to preach the gospel to the non-believing world. Jesus told His disciples in Matthew 28:19 to *"go and make disciples of all nations."*

Not all of us can go, but just because we don't go, we are no less responsible! We should have the same commitment to win the lost. You see, it is our responsibility to pray for the men and women who have answered the call.

"Devote yourselves to prayer, being watchful and thankful. And pray for us, too, that God may open a door for our message, so that we may proclaim the mystery of Christ, for which I am in chains. Pray that I may proclaim it clearly, as I should" (Colossians 4:2-4 NIV),

Paul's request to the Colossians rings as true to us today as it did to those first-century Christians. We cannot all go but we can all pray. And our prayers can powerfully affect the fields that are ripe for harvesting as well as fields where there is no work. Our prayers can pave the way and open doors.

7 ADOPTIVE INTERCESSOR

Do you have a deep concern for missions, for spreading the gospel throughout the world? Do you sincerely wish you could do something to impact our world? Do you want to make your time really count for something worthwhile? If your answer to any of these questions was "yes," then you need to become an adoptive intercessor.

Prayer can take you anywhere in the world and where prayer goes, so goes God. An adoptive intercessor adopts a city or country as his personal responsibility to intercede for a spiritual breakthrough. You may never physically visit your adopted city or country, but in prayer you can be there every day. Because you care, you will seek to know its conditions and situations so you can pray intelligently. This assigned intercession then becomes a regular part of your daily prayers.

See the world—through prayer!

8 IF I PERISH, I PERISH

Like many great characters in history, Esther made her first appearance as one of the humblest of figures, an orphan. But four years later she rose to the position of queen, a power she used wisely. Esther had been chosen queen in the time when wicked Haman, the king's second-in-command, sought to destroy all the Jews in the entire kingdom.

Haman convinced the king to issue a decree to wipe out the Jews. The king even gave Haman his signet ring to seal the decree. This was a very serious matter, because even the king himself could not revoke a decree sealed with the king's signet ring. A death sentence thus hung over the Jews as they waited for the date set by their enemy to kill them.

But there was a praying woman, an intercessor who fasted and prayed. She refused to sit idly by and do nothing. Esther earnestly sought God, crying out to Him as she persevered in effectual prayer. It was through this prayer that God intervened and gave her favor with the king and ultimately spared her people.

Serious times calls for serious measures. The situation looked bad. Esther could have easily lost her life and her people would have still died. But she refused to stand by and do nothing.

I have personally resigned that *"If I perish, I perish,"* but I will not sit by and watch souls be slaughtered by the enemy. I am going to touch God on their behalf, no matter the cost.

Have you considered that our prayers might be all that stands between souls and eternity? Join me today in earnest, effectual prayer for souls to be saved. I believe that our King will also give us favor and respond.

9 GETTING PAST WHAT I'LL NEVER GET OVER

I received a call from my friend Lois Allmon. We talked a while and then I asked Sister Allmon how she was doing. Two years prior, Brother Allmon, the love of her life, had collapsed in the pulpit while preaching and later passed away at the hospital. Sister Allmon, a faithful woman of prayer, responded, "Lisa, I am daily getting past what I will never get over."

I am an optimistic person. I prefer to see the glass half full. But the simple truth is there are things that happen in life that you may never get over—a traumatic event, the death of a parent or loved one, divorce, a hurt by a close friend . . . the list could go on. While we may not get over these things, with God's help and with prayer we can daily get past it.

No matter what has happened, God still gives peace that passes understanding. He is still with us through the valley of the shadow of death. He is still our provider, savior, and friend.

I must confess, sometimes I don't understand God. Job was a good person and it was his goodness that got him in an unbearable situation. Then to make matters worse, when Job asked God why, God's response was, "Job, where were you when I made the world? Job, what holds up the pillars that support the earth? Job, who do you think closed the gates to hold back the sea when it burst from the earth? Job, have you walked on the floor of the ocean?"

God asked Job over forty questions and Job couldn't answer a single one! I believe God was saying, "You will never understand Me. All you need to do is to realize how powerful I am and trust Me."

If you are carrying hurts today, take them to God in prayer. Let Him overwhelm you with His presence. Let Him surround you with His love and wrap you in His arms of peace and safety. He truly can help you get past what you may never get over.

10 JESUS, I KNOW

"Then certain of the vagabond Jews, exorcists, took upon them to call over them which had evil spirits the name of the Lord Jesus, saying, We adjure you by Jesus whom Paul preacheth. And there were seven sons of one Sceva, a Jew, and chief of the priests, which did so. And the evil spirit answered and said, Jesus I know, and Paul I know; but who are ye? And the man in whom the evil spirit was leaped on them, and overcame them, and prevailed against them, so that they fled out of that house naked and wounded" (Acts 19:13-16).

They had watched Paul. They knew what to do, what to say, and how to say it, so they assumed they could do what he did. However, they had no power! Without the power, they were just saying words, and it got them in trouble (not to mention, naked).

It is not enough to just know what to do and say in

19

prayer, but we must spend time daily building a relationship with God. When we are close to Him, we will have the power and authority to use that precious name. Since He is ours and we are His, He will respond.

11 WE MUST BE PEOPLE OF PRAYER

May I make a very bold statement?

You cannot be a Christian and not pray. It simply defies logic. To be Christ-like is following and adhering to the teachings of Jesus Christ. One thing was very clear about Jesus—He prayed!

He prayed at the beginning of His earthly ministry. Jesus prayed, the heaven was opened up, and the Spirit descended on Him like a dove. (See Luke 3:21-22.)

Jesus withdrew for a time of prayer. He often went on the mountainside to pray. He prayed late at night. (See Matthew 14:23.) He got up early to pray. (See Mark 1:35.) He prayed in the wilderness alone. (See Luke 5:16.)

Jesus prayed with others. In Luke 9:28, He took

21

Peter, James, and John and prayed.

Jesus spent time in prayer before making major choices. Before choosing the disciples, He spent the entire night praying. (See Luke 6:12-13.) I wonder how much better our lives would be if we spent all night praying before we made major choices?

Jesus prayed for others. *"Simon, Satan hath desired to have you, but I prayed for you that your faith fail not."* Jesus prayed for the disciples. (See Luke 22:32.)

Jesus often turned prayer times into teaching experiences. After a time of prayer with the disciples, Jesus asked, *"Who do people say that I am?"* (Luke 18-20). And revelation came to Peter: *"Thou art the Christ."*

Jesus prayed during His greatest time of need. Twice while on the cross, He prayed: *"Father, forgive them,"* and *"Into thy hands I commend my spirit."* (See Luke 23:34, 46.)

Jesus taught persistence in prayer. He told the disciples that men ought always to pray and not give up. (See Luke 18:1.) I can't imagine He would tell them to do something He wasn't doing himself.

Jesus prayed before meals. When He fed the five thousand with the boy's lunch of bread and fish (Mark 6:41); when he fed the four thousand (Mark

8:6); when He shared a meal with His disciples in the upper room the night before His crucifixion (Mark 14:22), and, following His resurrection, when He shared a meal with Cleopas and his wife in Emmaus (Luke 24:30).

If we are Christlike, then we must be people of prayer.

12 PRAYER

Prayer is what differentiates us from the rest of the religious world. The reason? Because we pray to a God who actually listens to us. Consider the story of Elijah when he mocked the prophets of Baal ("Go head and cut yourselves and scream louder"). It really didn't matter what they did because no one was listening. However, it was much different when Elijah prayed, because his God not only listened, but responded to his prayer.

The Bible states that our God is *"the same, yesterday, today, and forever."* Pray with confidence knowing that the God you serve hears and answers prayers today, tomorrow, and forever.

13 SUGGESTIONS

Many people have asked my advice on how to have a better prayer life. There is not a secret formula; it basically comes down to discipline. Here are a few suggestions to help you get started.

Don't just talk about prayer, pray! You may know everything there is to know about prayer but if you do not pray, you are not affecting the kingdom.

Schedule a prayer time. Setting aside time is the most important place to begin in developing your prayer life. If you never take time to pray, your prayer life will never grow. Make an appointment with God and keep it.

Create an environment for prayer. Choose a quiet place away from distractions.

Pace yourself. If you currently do not have an established prayer life, start small then build up to longer times of prayer.

Vary your prayer time activities. Pray with a list. Pray scriptures. Try different postures (kneeling, standing, walking, etc.) Pray about a different subject each day of the week. For example,

Monday: government leaders
Tuesday: family and friends
Wednesday: worldwide revival
Thursday: church and pastor
Friday: community
Saturday: the sick and disabled
Sunday: the elderly

Pray through the newspaper. Target different areas on different days by using a map of your city.

Pray for yourself and pray for others. The old adage says it well, 'They need the prayer and you need the practice.'

To enlarge your understanding and increase your desire, read some books on prayer that builds faith. The more you pray the more you will have a desire to pray. When you see the positive effects, you'll be hooked.

14 UNITY

Recently while my pastor was preaching a wonderful message on the subject of unity, the Lord brought to my mind the story of the friends who tore off the roof to get the man sick of the palsy to Jesus.

Something about this story was very interesting to me. I did not find where the sick friend actually asked his friends to do this or even voiced that he wanted to be taken to Jesus. Now, I can't imagine he wouldn't want to be healed, but I did not find it recorded that he made any such request. Obviously, the friends were demonstrating unity or they would have never been able to do what they did in removing the roof and lowering the sick man down to Jesus.

Could it be that when the church truly unifies, people who may not even be thinking about Jesus will be brought into His presence and have their lives changed? Could our unity ultimately get people into God's presence and produce a miracle for them even if they may not be looking for one?

Take time this week and pray for "the church" as well as "your church" to truly be unified, walking in the Spirit and listening for God's voice. Ask God to search your heart and let you be in unity with what He wants to do in your life and your sphere of influence.

15 DIVINE INTERRUPTIONS

I called a friend who works on staff at a church. There was no answer, so the call went to voicemail. A while later, my friend called back. She apologized for the delay in returning my call and went on to tell me that she in the middle of a church staff meeting, a prayer meeting had broken out. I listened as she told me the church leadership had been burdened for the country of Syria and were discussing how as a church they could help the country. In the middle of this discussion, they began to pray. It very soon turned into a deep, lengthy time of prayer.

I can't help but think it could only be a positive if more prayer meetings broke out in the middle of church staff meetings, Sunday school classes, counseling sessions, choir practices, and home friendship groups. I believe in doing things in order, but don't you think it pleases God during those times we are more concerned about following the leading of the Spirit than following our agendas or schedules?

Let me encourage you to stop and linger in God's presence when you feel that shift in the Spirit. Don't be in such a hurry to get back to the business at hand. What better business is there than spending time in God's presence?

16 THE NAME OF JESUS

One of my favorite songs of late is "Break Every Chain." It has been on repeat on my iPhone for some time now. It reminds me that there is power in that name that is above every name. While I am a fan of praise and worship music, I have noticed that many songs mention "Lord" and "God." While that is fine, I have to confess that there is something that connects with my heart when we sing about the name of Jesus.

In teaching children to pray, and often when I teach adults, I remind them to start their prayers "in the name of Jesus," end their prayers "in the name of Jesus," and put it in the middle as much as possible. For it is *that* name that has all power. It is *that* name that makes demons tremble. It is *that* name that we can run into and find safety.

Make an extra effort to call on the name of Jesus during your prayer time this week. Speak the name of Jesus over your family, over your community, over your church and your district. Speak that name over situations in your life that need a miracle. Speak the name of Jesus over someone that needs healing. It isn't a magic formula, but it is the most powerful name in the universe. When you speak His name, something *will* happen.

Call on the name of Jesus this week . . . and expect the miraculous.

17 KNOWING GOD'S WILL

A couple of years ago a young man that was in my prayer class at Gateway (now Urshan College) asked if I would pray for him. He had been asked to speak in chapel and was nervous about his message. Trying to be supportive, I told him that I would not only pray for him but I would come hear him speak. So I made my way to Gateway's chapel service the following morning.

I can't say that his message for the most part was all that spectacular. It was obvious that this was new for him and early in his speaking career. However, I was proud of his effort and the amount of prayer and preparation that had gone into it.

Then it happened.

He made a comment that impacted me beyond what I could describe in this intro. It was such a simple statement, yet so deeply profound. He simply said, "You know, we pray a lot asking God to show us His will for our lives. Not sure how we can expect to know God's will for our lives when we don't even know it for our day."

Wow!

Instantly I thought of how many times I skipped right past today, seeking God for the next bigger and better thing down the road. I wanted to know my future and would seek God diligently for direction, often ignoring my daily direction. Was I in church? Yes. Was I praying daily? Yes. But I often got the cart ahead of the horse, so to speak. God's Word says He will be a *"lamp to our feet."* A lamp only illuminates a couple of feet. I think we would prefer that God would be a headlight (showing a great distance ahead of us) rather than a lamp (showing only a short distance).

I hope to see that young man again one day and tell him that his message really did change my life. No longer do I seek God for the future. I seek God for today, knowing that if I follow His will each day, it will keep direct my life to the place He wants for me.

18 SISTER SCOTT

One of my favorite teachers in Bible school was Sister Joyce Scott. She was also by far, one of the hardest teachers I ever had during my time at Gateway. I grew very close to Sister Joyce Scott and through her friendship, which I will always consider a gift from God, I met her mother, Dorothy Scott. To me, Joyce Scott is now lovingly known as Abigail (long story) and her mom is known as Sister Scott. And today I want to tell you about Sister Scott.

I loved the elder Sister Scott from day one of meeting her. It probably had to do with the fact that our first encounter involved homemade biscuits and gravy, but even beyond that, I knew this lady was someone I wanted and needed in my life. You see, Sister Scott and I had a common interest, and it has showed up in most every conversation we have had. Not only do we share a love for good country cooking, but we share a love for prayer.

Sister Scott is in her eighties, so she has had forty-plus more years to practice prayer than I have, and I value her insight. I absolutely love to be with her. Without fail, I leave with a stronger faith in knowing what prayer can do. Her faith is contagious—but isn't that how it should be?

For Sister Scott, prayer isn't complicated. It is quite simple—her view is when God's people pray, something is going to happen! I am afraid that you have come too late to convince Sister Scott that prayer doesn't produce miracles. You've come too late to convince her that for any situation to change, you simply need to pray. You see, for many years, this faithful prayer warrior has seen God do the miraculous over and over again. She knows what happens when you sow in prayer, and reminds me every time I am privileged to be with her.

When I need prayer for something in my life and need to call out the big guns, Sister Scott instantly comes to mind. People like Dorothy Scott are like God's secret weapon against the enemy. I imagine you have a Sister Scott in your life as well and are thinking of her right now.

Why not take time this week and thank her for the impact she has had on your life.

Everyone needs a Sister Scott. I was blessed to have two.

19 IS THAT AN ANGEL I SEE?

""The angel fetched Peter out of prison, but it was prayer that fetched the angel." —*Thomas Watson*

So often when referencing the story of Peter in prison, we focus on the miracle of the angel coming to release him. After all, it was a pretty cool miracle. But Mr. Watson had it right—had prayer not gone forth, it is unlikely the angel would have made an appearance.

What situation in your life right now needs a miracle? Peter's situation looked pretty hopeless—*but prayer was made.*

No matter how big it looks, no matter how impossible it seems, when prayer is made, the miraculous instantly becomes possible. You may feel imprisoned. You may feel chained to things that have you bound. My suggestion to you—pray!

That prayer may be the very thing that brings your miracle.

Wait . . . is that an angel I see?

20 IT IS MY JOB TO PRAY

A kindergarten teacher was observing her classroom of children while they were drawing. She would occasionally walk around to see each child's work. As she got to one little girl who was working diligently, she asked what the drawing was. The girl replied, "I'm drawing God." The teacher paused and said, "But no one knows what God looks like." Without missing a beat, or looking up from her drawing, the girl replied, "They will in a minute!"

Don't you love the faith and confidence of a child? How sad that too few adults share that type of confidence when it comes to prayer. The truth of the matter is that we should just *know* that when we pray, something powerful is going to happen. We should know that as Spirit-filled Christians, when we do something according to God's will and have the help of His power that works within us, circumstances are going to change.

I heard a statement at a conference that I loved. The speaker said someone asked what happens if he prays for someone and nothing happens. The speaker simply said, "I pray for the next person." The concept was simple: it is my job to pray and God's job to answer. When I do my part, I fully expect Him to do His.

Will God answer as we want each time? No, probably not. But He *will* answer. It is our job to trust Him. I would venture to guess that if we stepped out in boldness a little more often, great things would happen much of the time.

James 5:16 says, *"The effectual, fervent prayer of a righteous man availeth much."* A more modern rendering says, *"When God's people pray, great things happen!"* I don't know about you, but I want to have confidence like that little girl and know that when I am done praying, things will be different.

21 HEZEKIAH

Hezekiah was a king of Judah. Jewish writings say he was one of Judah's best kings. His father was Ahaz, one of Judah's most wicked, ineffective kings.

When Ahaz finally died, Hezekiah inherited the damaged spiritual, economic, and political legacy his father left him. The nation was in debt. The people were broken in spirit. The country was in danger of being enslaved permanently to the Assyrians. And to make matters worse, Hezekiah was only twenty-five years old when he took the throne.

But Hezekiah had a three major things going his way:

1) he had a good mother, Abijah, daughter of the priest, Zechariah;

2) he had a preacher in his life, the prophet Isaiah; and

3) he had a prayer life.

The Bible records two bad situations in Hezekiah's life.

The Assyrian king was busy subduing nation after nation when he received a report that the Egyptian king was amassing an army and planning to march against him. Figuring he needed to consolidate his territory and secure his borders, he sent a letter to Hezekiah that basically said, "Don't think for one minute that your little god is going to save you from me. I'm pretty busy right now with this Egyptian thing, but if you know what's good for you, you'll just surrender. I will remind you that Assyria has dominated every other nation in this part of the world. None of their gods saved them and yours won't save you."

Hezekiah's response is my favorite part of this whole story. Hezekiah takes the letter to the Temple, lays it out on the floor, and prays,

"God, will You read this! Do You see what he's saying about You? He's insulting You! He's saying You aren't interested in us, that You aren't aware, and that You lack the power to do anything about his threats. He says You're just like the blind, deaf, and dumb idols of all the other nations. So God, I want You to deliver us from this maniac so that all the world will know that You alone are God."

Here we see Hezekiah doing the very thing Jews in the Old Testament were so good at—reminding God to be God. Hezekiah believed God was aware, involved, and powerful, and God always responds to that kind of faith. God responded immediately to Hezekiah's prayer: an angel struck the camp of the Assyrian army and 185,000 died. Their king fled home, only to be murdered by his sons.

The first thing we learn from Hezekiah is that if we pray, the Lord will fight our battles.

The most arresting words in this story are the words God addressed to Hezekiah: *"Because you have prayed to me."* This clearly implies that God would not have acted had Hezekiah not prayed.

In the second situation, Hezekiah became very sick and was at the point of death. The prophet Isaiah came to see him and told him to get his house in order because he was going to die. (Isn't that just the kind of encouraging words you want to hear from your pastor?) But Hezekiah turned his face to the wall and prayed. He shed tears and pleaded with God to help him.

"God, I beg You to remember how I've lived my life. I've lived faithfully in Your presence, and my heart has been totally dedicated to You." The Lord heard Hezekiah's prayers and granted him fifteen more years!

The second thing we learn from Hezekiah is that the faithful can ask for favors.

God doesn't owe us one thing. But there is nothing wrong with saying, "God, I am coming to You and I need Your help. I have been faithful to You for many years, and I need for You to be faithful to me right now."

22 A CONVERSATION WITH GOD

Prayer by definition is "a conversation with God." According to Webster, *conversation* is "an exchange of thoughts or information." So basically, prayer for believers should be an exchange of thoughts or information with God—a two-way communication where one party says something and the other responds.

Yet why is it so often when we pray, we are the only one talking?

My guess would be that often we don't hear from God because we are content to do all the talking and let Him do all the listening.

Do you know anyone who likes to talk a lot? You know the type—she talks non-stop from the moment you see her. She monopolizes the conversation and hardly comes up for air. You walk away feeling like your purpose wasn't really to converse, but rather to listen to her talk (and talk, and talk, and talk). Are you getting the picture? I wonder how many times we have done that to God.

The next time you pray, take a few minutes to be quiet. I have found it is very difficult to hear that "still small voice" while I am talking.

23 FIVE MINUTES PER DAY

George Barna reports the sobering statistic that most Christians pray less than five minutes per day.

Wow!

I am trying to picture in my mind how many marriages would survive with less than five minutes dialogue daily. How many relationships would become stronger or grow with that small and limited amount of communication? When you love someone, not only do you *want* contact with him, but I think it would be safe to say that you also *need* contact with him. For a relationship to grow and flourish, time must be spent in each other's presence. For a person to have a secure feeling in a relationship, there must be fellowship on a consistent basis.

In light of Mr. Barna's statistics, I ask, how much time are you spending with God? Only you and

God know the answer to that question.

Life is busy—at least mine is. Really busy! So often I find myself so busy with church and ministry that I miss out on time with the one I have committed my life to. It simply can't be this way. I have not pledged my life to ministry. I have not pledged my life to church. I have pledged my life to Jesus Christ. Ministry and church are a byproduct of my devotion to Him, but it can never replace my one-on-one time with the one I love most.

Starting today, let's live our lives in a way that if Mr. Barna came to my house or yours to visit, he would have to rewrite his statistics.

24 WISDOM FROM JOSH

I must confess, helping teach a kids prayer class has made me realize that I didn't know quite as much as I thought about prayer. I find myself being taught by them more and more.

A few weeks ago, we were teaching on the armor of God. I particularly liked this lesson because I have been a long-time advocate of praying the Word. One of the teachers was talking about using the sword of the Spirit. She mentioned what a powerful weapon it was when you began to pray the Word of God, using it to fend off the enemy or to attack offensively.

While I sat there deep in my own thoughts about the subject, one of the kids said something incredibly simple, yet incredibly powerful. Wide-eyed and connecting the dots in his young mind, Josh yelled out, "Yeah! And the devil don't have no armor, so our sword will take him out real fast!"

Wow! Suddenly I began to envision how helpless someone without armor would be if attacked by a sword. Josh was right—he wouldn't last long at all.

I know the enemy has power, but I think we sometimes forget how much *more* power God has. And if His Word is correct, *we* have that same power. Josh painted a picture in my mind and my heart that I won't soon forget. I don't have to be afraid of the enemy; he doesn't have any armor, but I do!

Next time the enemy bothers me, he's going down in a hurry. Thanks, Josh.

25 THAT FAMILIAR SOUND

I live in St. Louis, Missouri—in Florissant, to be exact. However, my mom would be quick to tell you that I am not from Missouri—I am from Alabama. Yes, it is true; my roots are planted deep in the South. My cell phone ringer plays the opening guitar part of "Sweet Home Alabama" and I say "y'all" whether I mean to or not, which is at least ten times a day. I am actually in Alabama now helping my mom with a few things and enjoying time with family and the slower pace of the good 'ole South. I am happy. I now get to wave at everyone I pass on the road without anyone looking at me strange.

A couple of nights ago I went to my room to go to bed. I have been away from home over twenty years but I still have my room. I hurried, got in bed, and waited for it. I knew it would come at any moment. Yes! There it was! Permeating through my bedroom walls came that familiar sound that I love so much to hear.

I was home. Let me explain.

On the other side of the wall where my bed sits is the closet to another bedroom. In that closet is the most valuable item existing on the nine acres that Mom lives on, and possibly the entire city (if you can call the metropolis of Green Pond a city, that is). It is a piece of furniture, a priceless artifact. The closet it sits in is no ordinary closet; it is my mother's prayer room. That priceless artifact is an old chair that most people would not give $.50 for at a garage sale, but it is at that chair that my mother daily kneels to pray.

I hurried to my bed that night because I knew I would hear that sweet sound echoing through the walls, saturating my room with hope and faith . . . and I did. You see, as sure as the sun comes up in the morning and as sure as the moon shows its face at night, it's sure that my mom will pray before going to bed, when she gets up, before every meal, and all through the day. I've listened to that sound my entire life; it's priceless to me.

Moms and dads, by what memories will your children remember you? I heard a message this past weekend which talked about us being "epistles read of all men." I can tell you for sure that when you read the book of Barbara Allen, my sweet, precious mother, you will read a book about prayer.

26 FRIENDS

Statistics show that in 2013, the average number of friends that most people had on Facebook is around three hundred.

We are friends with people we rarely (and sometimes, never) see or maybe don't even know. We only want short quips and quotes, or photos that we can quickly glance at and share. Family members now write posts or personal message each other on Facebook or text each other as they sit in the same house.

More and more, we no longer take the time or spend the effort to develop deep relationships. Although technology has changed—and it is constantly changing—God has not. He still requires a relationship.

Take time this week to spend time getting to know

the one you have dedicated your life to serve. Close Facebook and Twitter and spend uninterrupted time alone with God. Talk to Him and allow time for Him to talk to you.

27 A SPIRIT OF PRAYER

Each Monday evening I help teach a kids prayer class at my church. Last night, I decided to go upstairs and pray with the adults. We have a fairly new saint in our church who recently relocated to St. Louis to be near her family. Her name is Sister Esther Weeks and she is 83 years old. During the prayer meeting, my attention was instantly captivated by Sister Esther.

As the person leading prayer led us to pray for different things, I watched as the group prayed and eventually stopped to wait on the next thing to pray about. But not Sister Esther! After everyone's prayer had run its course, Sister Esther was still praying. It did not phase her at all that everyone had stopped. She continued her prayer—and what a prayer it was! Her prayer was filled with faith and passion. It became very apparent to me that she is the epitome of a seasoned prayer warrior; without a doubt, there was a spirit of prayer on her. It impacted me in a way that I'm not even sure I can express.

You see, I remember as a child listening to my grandmother and my Aunt Mae pray that way. I have to confess there were times I thought they would never stop praying. I would give anything to be able to go back and listen to them again. As a child, I really had no idea how blessed I was to be exposed to that type of praying. The type of praying that was from a very deep place and was rock-solid in faith that God would hear and respond.

My prayer last night before going to bed: "God, please let the same spirit of prayer fall on me and my generation that Sister Esther has." That gut-wrenching prayer that grips your heart and won't let go. The type of prayer that presses you to go farther than most and keep praying after silence has fallen on the room. I believe it is that type of effectual, fervent prayer that moves mountains and shakes the foundation of hell.

Thank you, Sister Esther, for being an example to those of us coming along behind you.

28 YOUTH

Oh, to be young again! I remember when I was in my teens and early twenties, it seemed like I could go days without sleep. I basically lived on Mountain Dew, barbecue chips, and chicken fingers, and had limitless energy. (I also wore several sizes smaller clothes than I do now.) Oh, to be young again.

Young people are the church's most valuable, natural resource. Their energy, creativity, and mission-mindedness are needed if the church is going to realize its potential and perpetuate the apostolic message. This energy must be directed constructively, which can only be done by seeking God. Satan wants to turn youthful energy into a negative, destructive force. We must, however, challenge his desire through focused intercession for our youth.

George Barna says three out of four youth are

leaving the church when they turn eighteen and never return. I firmly believe that prayer can change this statistic. Join me this week and pray for the youth in your life. Call them by name. Pray for your children. Pray for the youth in your neighborhood. Pray for the youth in your church. But then pray bigger. Pray for all youth. Pray for trends happening with young people. Pray for the broad scale temptations that youth face. Pray for the next generation to be strong. And then send a few cards and let them know you are praying and believe in them.

29 CHALLENGES IN PRAYER

If someone were to ask what the greatest challenge the World Network of Prayer (where I work) has is, two things would instantly come to mind.

Without a doubt our biggest challenge is trying to raise people's focus of prayer. You see, most feel prayer is the means by which we ask God for something we need. And while we do make our requests known, that is *not* the primary reason we pray. The main reason we pray is because we love the one we are praying to and want to get closer.

Remember when you first met your sweetheart? There weren't enough hours in the day to talk to him. In order to grow in relationship with someone, you have to get to know him and that happens by spending time with him.

The second challenge would be getting people to

understand the importance of getting quiet when they pray. Most spend their entire time in prayer doing all the talking, when what they should do is spend part of their time listening.

I fear many Christians walk around frustrated due to unanswered questions in their life, when the sad truth is God wants to answer them but they never get quiet long enough to allow Him to speak.

Many also get frustrated feeling they don't pray long enough. That hour goal might be less intimidating if you feel you didn't have to spend the entire hour doing all the talking.

Take time this week and raise your focus of prayer. Pray for a missionary, a nation, people groups, those in false religions, the finances of kingdom work, orphans, the addicted . . . and so on. Better yet, get quiet and ask God what He wants you to pray about. Let Him dictate your prayer time this week. He might have something He wants to say to you. Get quiet and see.

30 ANTONIN SCALIA

This past weekend Associate Supreme Court Justice Antonin Scalia died in his sleep at a hunting resort in West Texas. Having served almost thirty years on the bench, Justice Scalia was the longest serving member of the current Supreme Court. He was also one of the most conservative justices the US has ever had. His career was defined by his reverence for the constitution and his legacy of protecting Americans' most cherished freedoms.

The Supreme Court has long been divided. There are four liberal judges (Ginsburg, Breyer, Kagan, and Sotomayor) and four conservatives (Thomas, Roberts, Alito, and Scalia) with the swing vote being Anthony Kennedy, who tends to lean more conservative than liberal.

Why the civics lesson today? Because it is imperative that you and I pray for the justice who will fill Justice Scalia's place. The appointment of another liberal justice could swing the majority of the court to the side of the liberals, who give little or no value to religious rights.

Will you join me and earnestly pray for the person who will replace Justice Scalia? Ask God to give us someone with a conservative agenda. Someone who will seek righteousness. Someone not afraid to take a stand godliness and protect the things that you and I hold so dear. Someone who will stand for the right as Justice Scalia did for thirty years.

I exhort therefore, that, first of all, supplications, prayers, intercessions, and giving of thanks, be made for all men; For kings, and for all that are in authority; that we may lead a quiet and peaceable life in all godliness and honesty (I Timothy 2:1-2, emphasis mine).

31 ONE IS ALL YOU NEED

One day I decided to look up how many Scripture verses referred to "do not fear" or "fret not." The first article I found said there were 365 verses. I was thrilled—one for each day. Then I read something that said many of them were a different context than someone who was going through a trial or difficult time. I was disappointed. But then I read one sentence that put it all in perspective for me: "What does it matter? If God said it once, isn't that enough?"

What an eye opener for me. There was stinging truth in that sentence. If God said it one time, that should be more than enough for us.

"Do not be anxious about anything, but in everything by prayer and supplication with thanksgiving let your requests be made known to God. And the peace of God, which surpasses all

understanding, will guard your hearts and your minds in Christ Jesus" (Philippians 4:6-7).

Whatever circumstance you are facing today, find comfort in the fact that God has given many promises in His Word that He will be with you. Although there are many, truthfully, *one* is all you need.

32 VICTORY

In the Book of Judges, Gideon taught us that if we want to win the battle, we must first start the battle on our knees. Facing impending danger, Gideon's word of faith to the three hundred made an impactful difference.

He returned to the camp of Israel and said, "*Arise, for the Lord has given the camp of Midian into your hands.*" We are going in knowing in advance the Lord has given us the victory.

Talk about faith! Gideon resolved to go and claim what was already his. Gideon was not fighting *for* victory but *from* victory. The Lord had already given him the victory; it was his job to claim it—not to figure out how it would happen, not to help facilitate it. He simply had to go get what was his.

March through life knowing God has positioned you to win. You are not fighting *for* victory, but *from* victory. There are over eight thousand promises in the Bible available to you through Jesus Christ. Plant yourself on the Word of God and His promises and see what God does in your life.

33 THANKFUL

Have you paused recently to consider all that you have to be thankful for? It is important for each of us to make a habit of taking time to consider all the blessings God has bestowed upon us.

We each have gifts and abilities, and we each have experiences and knowledge that enable us to make a unique contribution in our families, churches, communities, and world. Together we share an awesome responsibility and opportunity. We have the ability to impact the whole world with our prayers.

There have been terrorist attacks in several locations and the impending threat of many more from ISIS and others. But may I borrow wisdom from Elisha in 2 Kings 6:16? *"And he answered, Fear not: for they that be with us are more than they that be with them."* A more modern translation says, *"Don't be afraid! There are more on our side than on theirs!"*

During this time, let your heart be at peace and focus on what is for us. For we know, *"If God be for us, who can be against us?"*

34 THE SECRET PLACE

He who dwells in the secret place of the Most High shall remain stable and fixed under the shadow of the Almighty [Whose power no foe can withstand]" (Psalm 91:1, Amplified*).*

In Psalm 91 is a litany of amazing promises. Many believe that Psalm 91 has probably the most protective broad-scope promises found anywhere in Scripture. In summary, Psalm 91 says if you and I will take some care as to where we place ourselves, then God will unleash divine protection. But it is all conditional on verse one.

But notice, the protection and benefits flow from a decision of placement you and I make in our lives.

Where are you dwelling or placing yourself daily?

Are you dwelling in that secret place? Are you spending time daily with the Master?

If not, let me encourage you to change this. In this day and time, we desperately need the supernatural protection that is promised when we dwell in that secret place with Him.

35 PRAY FIRST

There is something that absolutely blows my mind. I will *never* understand how someone who is a Holy Ghost-filled Christian can make major decisions in life and never ask God His opinion. Marriage, a house purchase, a career change, a church change . . . you get the idea.

You have no idea how many times people have asked me for prayer while telling me of the horrific circumstance they found themselves in because of a decision they made. And more often than not when I would ask if they had prayed about it, they embarrassingly said "no."

If we would learn to get alone with God in the secret place of prayer when we have an important decision, then I am quite certain we would have much less heartache in life.

Do you know what Jesus did when it came time for Him to choose the twelve disciples, those who would change the world? He got alone in prayer. As a matter of fact, it was so important, He prayed all night.

Before you make any major decisions, might I recommend that you spend a night in prayer?

There will be times the answers we get in prayer will be difficult to receive. Do you realize the choice of Judas, who would later betray Jesus, was bathed in prayer? Jesus knew Judas would eventually betray Him. He wasn't surprised when it happened—but Jesus trusted the direction He found in the secret place of prayer. And we have to trust the answer too, even when we don't understand it.

Ask God before making decisions in your life. Let Him guide you in what you do. God doesn't simply want to get you on the right path; He wants to enjoy the journey with you.

36 AN AMBASSADOR FOR CHRIST

"The only thing necessary for the triumph of evil is for good men to do nothing." ~ Edmund Burke

In my opinion, for far too long the church has taken a passive role when it comes to politics. I guess I have to be honest and forthcoming to tell you that I don't really believe it is possible to separate church and state. You see, the Bible says, *"I exhort therefore, that, first of all, supplications, prayers, intercessions, and giving of thanks, be made for all men; for kings, and for all that are in authority; that we may lead a quiet and peaceable life in all godliness and honesty. For this is good and acceptable in the sight of God our Saviour"* (I Timothy 2:1-3).

With this being said, I feel it is a mandate to Christians to pray for our government and our leaders as well as policies and laws that impact our society.

Many important issues are being presented in both state and national government right now that can profoundly impact our lives as well as the church. We must pray! But along with prayer our voice needs to be heard. Let me encourage you to get involved. Vote! Write your representatives and let them know as a constituent, you trust they will make godly and wise decisions for your state or district.

As a Christian and "Ambassador for Christ," I want to do all I can. Will you join me?

37 LIFE IS BUSY

Life is busy. Sometimes it is *too* busy. Like most others, when I am the busiest, I struggle the most in finding time for God.

How ironic that often the thing I busy myself with is the work of God. But it is never acceptable to neglect the God of the work while working for God.

Take time this week to set aside alone time with God.

Here are a few suggestions:

1 Choose a quiet place away from distractions

2 Have inspirational material

3 Put on a worship CD

4 Have a Bible

5 Have a list of missionaries

6 Have a notepad in case God speaks something
to you or you think of something you need
to do

7 Make the decision to not let anything disrupt your
time with God

Take the time.

God misses His time with you.

38 THINGS I'VE LEARNED ABOUT PRAYER

The more you pray, the more you pray.

When I make my prayers about the Kingdom, my needs usually get taken care of also.

Volume does not equal anointing.

In the Bible, the fire of God never fell on an empty altar. Sometimes sacrifice is the key to a miracle.

Prayer partners are needed for every Christian.

Sometimes the best prayer times are when I don't say a word.

During prayer, I should listen more than I should talk.

My day should always start with prayer. My day should always end with prayer. (And I should pray in the middle as much possible.)

Daily consistency is a must.

There isn't just one way to pray. Pray how God made you to pray, be it quiet or loud.

"Effectual" and "fervent" have different meanings for different people.

ABOUT THE AUTHOR

Lisa Marshall has worked in prayer ministry for many years, and has traveled extensively teaching and speaking on the subject of prayer.

.

Made in the USA
Middletown, DE
16 March 2022

62725572R00050